Looking After Me

Teeth

Crabtree Publishing Company

www.crabtreebooks.com

Crabtree Publishing Company

www.crabtreebooks.com   1-800-387-7650

Published in Canada
Crabtree Publishing
616 Welland Ave.
St. Catharines, ON
L2M 5V6

Published in the United States
Crabtree Publishing
PMB16A
350 Fifth Ave., Suite 3308
New York, NY 10118

Senior editor
Jennifer Schofield

Designer
Sophie Pelham

Digital color
Carl Gordon

Editor
Molly Aloian

Copy editor
Adrianna Morganelli

Proofreader
Crystal Sikkens

Project coordinator
Robert Walker

Production coordinator
Margaret Amy Salter

Prepress technician
Katherine Kantor

First published in 2008 by Wayland
338 Euston Road
London NW1 3BH

Wayland Australia
Level 17/207 Kent Street
Sydney NSW 2000

Copyright © Wayland 2008

Wayland is a division of
Hachette Children's Books,
a Hachette Livre UK company.

Library and Archives Canada Cataloguing in Publication

Gogerly, Liz
    Teeth / Liz Gogerly ; illustrator, Mike Gordon.

(Looking after me)
Includes index.
ISBN 978-0-7787-4115-2 (bound).--ISBN 978-0-7787-4122-0 (pbk.)

    1. Teeth--Juvenile fiction. 2. Teeth--Care and hygiene--Juvenile
fiction. I. Gordon, Mike II. Title. III. Series: Gogerly, Liz.
Looking after me.

PZ7.G56Te 2008   j823'.92   C2008-903643-3

Library of Congress Cataloging-in-Publication Data

Gogerly, Liz.
    Teeth / written by Liz Gogerly ; illustrated by Mike Gordon.
        p. cm. -- (Looking after me)
    Includes index.
    ISBN-13: 978-0-7787-4122-0 (pbk. : alk. paper)
    ISBN-10: 0-7787-4122-2 (pbk. : alk. paper)
    ISBN-13: 978-0-7787-4115-2 (reinforced library binding : alk. paper)
    ISBN-10: 0-7787-4115-X (reinforced library binding : alk. paper)
    1. Teeth--Care and hygiene--Juvenile literature. 2. Deciduous teeth--
Juvenile literature. I. Gordon, Mike, ill. II. Title. III. Series.

RK63.G64 2009
617.6'01--dc22
                                    2008025365

Looking After Me

Teeth

Written by Liz Gogerly
Illustrated by Mike Gordon

I love my dog Billy. Whenever he was good, I gave him doggy chocolate treats and cookies.

One day when Billy was yawning,
I saw something black in his mouth.

It's a rotten tooth!

Rotten: Bad

6

We took Billy to the vet. He needed to have the bad tooth taken out!

The vet said that he shouldn't eat any more chocolate and he gave us a dog toothbrush and toothpaste.

Billy hated having his teeth
cleaned, but we didn't want
him to loose any more of them.

He needed his
teeth to eat,

to chew
Dad's slippers,

and to keep his tongue in place!

Instead of chocolates, we gave Billy juicy bones.

Soon he had sparkly white teeth and healthy pink gums.

11

But I didn't.

My front tooth was wobbling.
Very soon, it was going to fall out.

I didn't want a gap like Billy's.

Nor did I want all my teeth to rot.

I definitely didn't want any of Billy's chicken-flavored toothpaste.

Mom told me not to worry.

She said that
as we grow
older our baby
teeth fall out.

Our new adult teeth must last forever, so it's important that we look after them.

You should brush your teeth with fluoride toothpaste every morning and night.

when should you brush your teeth?

Food and drinks leave a sticky layer of white stuff on your teeth, called plaque.

Plaque and sugar
make your teeth decay.

When you brush
your teeth, you
get rid of the
plaque and sugar.

This helps
keep your
teeth and
gums healthy.

Decay = Like
rotten bad

I've discovered that teeth are amazing things. They are covered with a hard layer called enamel.

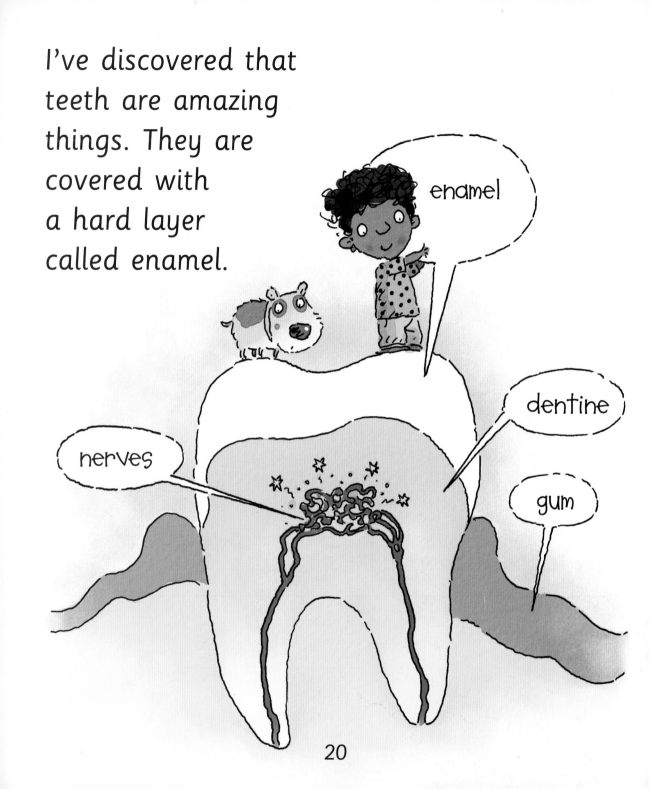

You also have different kinds of teeth.

You have canines for tearing, incisors for cutting, and molars for chewing.

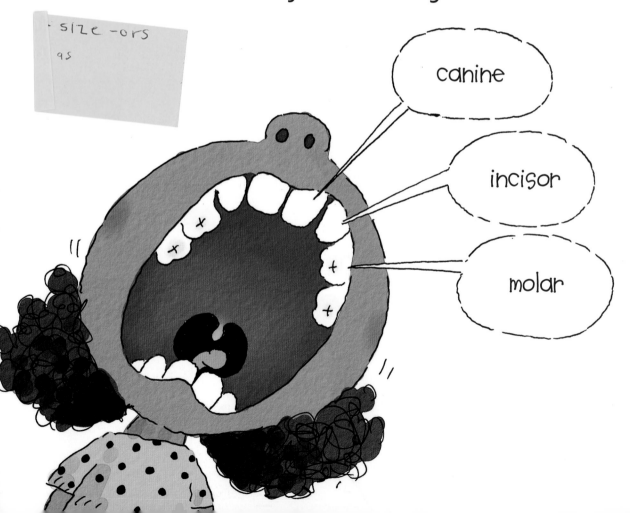

You must look after your teeth.
It all begins with brushing.

Mom buys me a
new toothbrush
every three months.

I never ever share my
brush with anyone!

23

Now I visit the dentist regularly.
She checks my teeth for decay.

If you have a bad tooth then your dentist may need to give you a filling.

Eating healthy food is also important for looking after your teeth.

At snack time I eat fruit,

vegetables, or cheese.

I drink water, especially
between meals.

If I have a sugary drink,
I use a straw.

Now, when a tooth falls out,
I don't worry anymore.

I pop it under my
pillow and wait
for the tooth fairy
to leave me a
shiny new coin!

NOTES FOR PARENTS AND TEACHERS

SUGGESTIONS FOR READING
LOOKING AFTER ME: TEETH
WITH CHILDREN

In this story, we meet a young girl, Marta, who learns that part of living a healthy lifestyle is learning about our teeth and how we look after them properly. Not looking after our teeth can lead to rotten teeth or fillings. In this story, it is Marta's dog, Billy, who suffers from a bad tooth. The idea of a dog needing dental treatment and having its teeth cleaned may be quite amusing for children. It is also a good way to initiate discussion about what the children think causes dental decay. Billy has been eating too many chocolates. The children will probably pick up on this. They may also have their own ideas about why Billy has a bad tooth.

Once Billy's tooth is removed, the vet instructs Marta to brush his teeth. This is a good opportunity to discuss the importance of cleaning our teeth twice a day. The American Dental Health Association (ADA) gives advice about how to brush children's teeth, as well as other useful information about looking after teeth at: www.ada.org. The ADA also suggests that children need assistance in cleaning their teeth until they are at least seven years old. You could point out that Billy has to be helped to clean his teeth.

Losing our first teeth, or baby teeth, is part of childhood. Unfortunately, Marta is confused and thinks that a wobbly tooth is a rotten tooth. The book aims to reassure children that losing their first teeth is normal and that these first teeth are replaced by adult teeth, which must last a lifetime. This is a good point to start talking about visiting the dentist for regular check-ups.

The text is filled with ways in which we can care for our teeth and perhaps the children have some ideas of their own. Together with the children, you could come up with a list of new resolutions to look after their own teeth.

LOOKING AFTER ME AND CURRICULUM EXPECTATIONS

The Looking After Me series is designed to teach young readers the importance of personal hygiene, proper nutrition, exercise, and personal safety. This series supports key K-4 health education standards in Canada and the United States, including those outlined by the American Association for Health Education. According to these standards, students will

- Describe relationships between personal health behaviors and individual well being
- Explain how childhood injuries and illnesses can be prevented or treated
- Identify responsible health behaviors
- Identify personal health needs
- Demonstrate strategies to improve or maintain personal health
- Demonstrate ways to avoid and reduce threatening situations

BOOKS TO READ

I Know Why I Brush My Teeth Kate Rowan (Walker Books, 2000)
Why Must I Brush My Teeth? Jackie Gaff (Cherrytree Books, 2004)
My Wobbly Tooth Must Not Ever Never Fall Out
Lauren Child (Puffin Books, 2006)

ACTIVITY

This activity can be done as a class project or individually. Children look for pictures of different animals in which they can see the animals' teeth. They then need to guess what kind of food the animals eat by looking at the teeth. For example, lions are carnivores and their teeth are sharp and suited to eating meat, while cows are herbivores and so have large, flat teeth, suitable for eating grass.

INDEX

Printed in China